Sacramento River

Sacramento River

Chip O'Brien

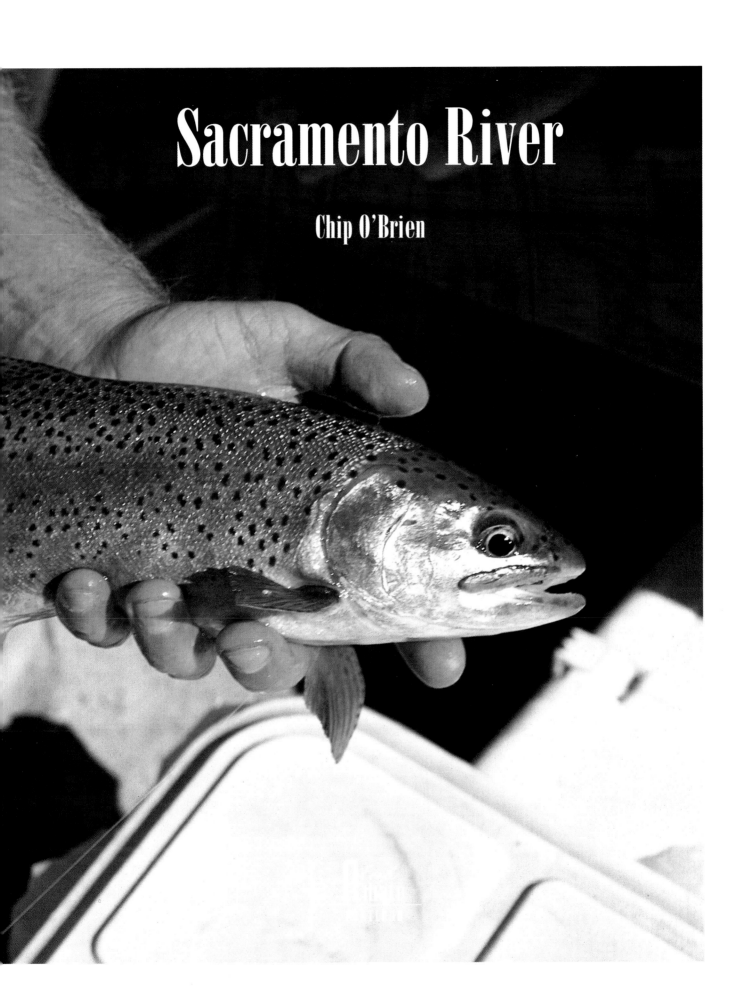

River Journal

Volume 4, Number 2, 1996

About the Author

Chip O'Brien was ten years old when he decided to fly fish and learn to write about it. Aside from a dubious 14-year digression in corporate sales, today he is doing just that. He moved his family to Redding in the 1980s, minutes from the Sacramento River, into the heart of California's best trout fishing.

During the season Chip works as a fishing guide and teaches adult and children's fly fishing classes. He is a columnist for *Western FlyFishing* Magazine and a regular contributor to *California Fly Fisher*.

Deeply concerned with preserving and enhancing quality public fishing opportunities, Chip has worked as a volunteer, regional manager and consultant for California Trout.

◆

Acknowledgments

Many thanks to Mark Stopher, Steve Turick and Mike Berry with California Department of Fish and Game for help on the Upper Sac; George Durand, Art Teter and Ernie Denison, fellow guides for sharing their knowledge of the lower Sac; Andy Burk and The Fly Shop for their terrific flies; Garth and the Big Fisherman.

◆

Series Editor: Frank Amato—Kim Koch

Subscriptions:
Softbound: $35.00 for one year (four issues)
$65.00 for two years
Hardbound Limited Editions: $95.00 one year, $170.00 for two years
Frank Amato Publications, Inc. • P.O. Box 82112 • Portland, Oregon 97282 • (503) 653-8108

Design: Alan Reid
Photography: Chip O'Brien & Portions from California State Archives
Map: Alan Reid
Printed in Hong Kong
Softbound ISBN:1-57188-051-8, Hardbound ISBN:1-57188-052-6
(Hardbound Edition Limited to 500 Copies)

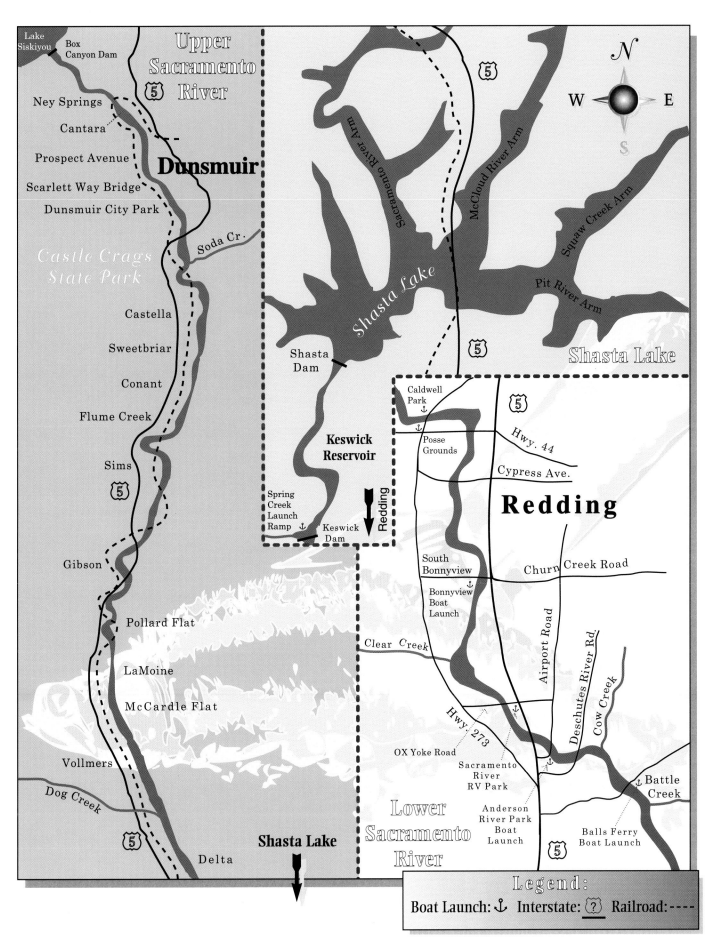

Sacramento River

THE SACRAMENTO RIVER

I've always felt that instinct is a perfectly acceptable reason for setting the hook. My pet theory held true today as the skyward jerk of my rod met with wild thrashing deep in the vicinity of my terminal tackle. "Fish on!"

The day was typical for late August on the Upper Sacramento River in that you could incinerate bacon and eggs on the streamside rocks if you wanted to. A featureless blue sky absorbed the herky-jerky rumblings of the occasional freight train up the canyon mingled with the distant drone of a super-highway, massive U.S. Interstate 5, from the bridge high overhead. Thorny vines laden with ripe blackberries groped down into the water presenting an angler with the happy dilemma to eat or to fish. Both seem equally appealing.

My friend Garth had chosen to head upstream while I worked down from where we had parked the truck; the rough plan being to rendezvous somewhere around lunch time. Having similar fishing preferences, I knew my friend realized we were probably crazy in thinking we could actually catch trout in the 105 degree heat of the Northern California summer. But I also knew that, like myself, sometimes Garth's reasons for needing to fish had very little to do with catching anything. Today was one of those days.

Experienced anglers in these parts know the best way to explore the Upper Sac is by hiking the adjacent railroad tracks to remote areas of the river, but today I gave in to the temptation to scramble down on the bedrock outcroppings in front of me in hopes of spotting some fish. The water is clear as a vodka tonic and, for an ardent angler, similarly intoxicating. I headed for the section above where a short riffle plunged white water into deep uncertainty. Big fish water. But in such beautiful places concentration can be an illusive thing.

First the crash of an osprey not practicing catch and release distracted me. Then railroad smells, creosote and diesel smoke, carried me back to a teenage summer I had spent working in a switching yard while the boss sipped bourbon all day in an air conditioned truck. Ruddy-looking men waved at me from open freight cars heading for who-knows-where.

At once my reel let out a shriek as the fish peeled off 30 feet of fly line in all of two seconds, leaped free of the water and popped my tippet with a twang like a too-tight banjo string. Then all was quiet.

"These fish are like that," nodded Garth between mouthfuls of sandwich. That was all he said. Despite the heat, my hands shivered.

IF YOU DON'T LIKE THE WATER, WAIT A WEEK...

Northern California's Sacramento River system is huge, diverse and unique in terms of both water types and fishing opportunities. The scope of this book encompasses over sixty miles of running water between the upper and lower Sacramento Rivers, as well as close to 300 miles of reservoir shoreline between Shasta Lake and Keswick Reservoir. All of it,

Kayakers take advantage of high springtime flows on the upper Sacramento River.

◆

thankfully, is first-class fly fishing water with streams containing thousands of fish per mile and a fish biomass in the reservoirs measured in tons per square acre.

But beyond being merely massive and varied, the system is also constantly changing as water levels expand and recede throughout the year. Both man and nature play a role in keeping the Sacramento ecosystem in a constant state of flux. Knowing a thing or two about what to expect at various times of the year is an essential aid in not wasting valuable fishing time chasing wild geese. It's every bit as important for an angler to develop a sense of where not to be at a given time, as it is to be able to pinpoint the best fishing throughout the year.

THE UPPER SACRAMENTO RIVER

Although the Sacramento River begins as two trickling forks that feed the impoundment named Lake Siskiyou, the classic fishing water begins where the combined flows bubble out from beneath Box Canyon Dam southwest of the town of Mount Shasta. Flowing mainly from north to south, the 38 miles of flowing water between Box Canyon Dam and massive Shasta Lake is known as the "upper" Sacramento River, and is considered by many to be the premier Northern California wild trout stream. And considering the overall quality of other streams in the vicinity, this is saying a lot.

Opening Day of general fishing season in California is the last Saturday in April and flows on the upper Sac can be, depending on the accumulated snowpack, four to five feet higher than flows later in the season. The weather this time of year is usually quite appealing; temperatures in the mid 70's or 80's under a powder blue sky. Only the high flows of the river betray signs of the previous rainy winter.

One thing you will notice about the upper Sac is the staggering clarity of the water. This, by the way, can be quite deceiving for the hapless wading angler enthusiastic to stick a few early season trout. The water is usually deeper than it appears, almost beckoning an angler to wade just a little deeper.

The river becomes fishable earliest toward the upper end where flows are considerably lower than down toward Shasta Lake. Minimum flows below the dam average about 40 cubic feet per second (cfs) creating a classic small stream fishery. After flowing almost forty miles and taking in snowmelt from at least ten major tributaries, low water flows at Dog Creek will average about 235 cfs. So you see, just pick the kind of trout water you like to fish and the upper Sac undoubtedly has it somewhere.

If the preceding winter was unusually wet or cold, a good early season tactic is to fish the upper river in the rugged gorge just below Lake Siskiyou. Access here is limited, but if you're willing to wear some of the felt from your wading boots, chances are that you can locate some remote water surrounded by towering granite peaks. Here the stream is narrow but configured in the standard riffle-run-pool, riffle-run-pool that becomes the hallmark of this beautiful fishery throughout its length. Wild, native rainbow trout can be easily seen in all the likely places offering the delightful opportunity to fish to visible fish.

Another good opening gambit is to locate almost any tributary to the upper Sac and fish around the confluence. High water often creates wide runs and deep pools where these smaller streams back up against the higher flows of the main stem of the river. Trout seem to be attracted to these spots where abundant food is plentiful and they don't have to fight the raging flows of the main river.

Another incredible feature of the upper Sac is that almost the entire river runs adjacent and parallel to the busiest north-south traffic thoroughfare on the west coast, sprawling U.S. Interstate 5. Virtually any exit off this superhighway between Shasta Lake to the south and the town of Mount Shasta to the north will put you within a few minutes of prime trout water. And if a major superhighway weren't enough, all but the top few miles of this stream is also closely paralleled by railroad tracks allowing almost unlimited access to those willing to walk a little. Though it might seem to some an unlikely mixture, the determined chugging of trains up and down the river seems to add an irresistible ambiance found in few other places.

Surprisingly few anglers are willing to walk the tracks in search of remote fishing. In a state with a population in the tens of millions, it seems outrageous that so few are willing to hike even a scant ten minutes to get away from designated parking areas. On this particular day Garth headed downstream and I went up.

By the looks of the water right in front of me, I could tell that any reasonable angler would pick this spot to start fishing. It was too perfect. The riffle had a moderate speed and about a four-foot depth with loads of boulders creating trout motels as far as the eye could see. Running right up the middle was a bedrock formation bisecting the water evenly; one stretch easily accessed, the other requiring some effort. I decided to go for the tough water.

Department of Fish and Game personnel were out in force as usual that day conducting a survey on angler success. One creel checker was there to meet Garth and I when we rendezvoused back at the truck, wanting to know how we had done. Garth, good fisherman that he is, made the mistake of going first announcing that he had landed four fish that afternoon. I honestly wasn't trying to make him feel bad when I reported the 21 fish I had caught, but some guys simply have no sense of humor.

By around mid-June, flows are usually down to normal summer conditions where they stay for the remainder of the season. Almost every inch of the river is easily fished from here on out.

SHASTA LAKE

One of the largest and grandest reservoirs on the west coast is Shasta Lake. When the lake is full it boasts 270 miles of shoreline and 29,500 acre feet of water. Too much water, you say? Leave it for the Budweiser Bass Fishing Team, you say? Well fly fishers shouldn't be too quick to declare Shasta unfishable, and are in a great position to take advantage of fluctuating water conditions.

The seasonal fluctuation of Shasta Lake follows the typical weather pattern for this part of the country. The area gets very little precipitation throughout most of the year. But what it gets, it gets all at once. The rains tend to fall somewhere between November and March, and it will rain "full tilt" for weeks on end. Most years find the lake full in the spring and then it is gradually drawn down over the dry season. The lake is usually at its lowest by September, allowing anglers with a preference for wading a unique opportunity. The lake can fluctuate as much as 100 feet or more from season to season.

When the lake is full, principally in the winter and spring in dry years, the usual angling tactics apply. Since these are described fully elsewhere in this book, let's restrict this discussion to low-water, late-season conditions.

Shasta was formed when a dam was built below the confluence of four great rivers: the Sacramento, McCloud, Squaw Creek and the Pit River. When the lake is full boaters can motor miles up these tributaries and have access to seemingly unlimited numbers of remote coves and bays within which to fish. But when the lake level drops in late summer, water that was once lake turns miraculously back into running water creating terrific opportunities to fish beautiful, remote and productive water left alone by most Shasta Lake anglers. This is water just

◆

Although considered part of Shasta Lake, the Pit River arm begins just above Fenders Ferry Road and offers year-round trout fishing and river-like conditions. (Watch out! The water levels here are subject to rapid fluctuation.)

Railroad bridge over the lower Sac in Redding showing winter low-water conditions.

◆

made for the wading fly fisher.

And few people take advantage of these conditions. It's understandable why most boaters prefer to fish deeper water from the comfort of their watercraft, but they are really (sorry) missing the boat. A great tactic is to motor up as far as you comfortably can, park your boat and walk the banks until you find wadable water. These areas hold abundant populations of both wild stream fish and large, Shasta Lake hatchery fish. Whichever you are able to connect with, the fishing can be really outstanding. In all the years I've been fishing this running lake water, I've seen very few anglers and never once could I have described these locations as crowded.

Another successful tactic for boatless anglers is to hike into these areas from the nearest road access. This usually isn't difficult. One of my favorites is the McCloud river arm, since Gilman Road (an exit off U.S. Interstate 5) closely parallels the water for miles in an area that is frequently turned into running water. There are numerous turnouts 15-20 miles off the freeway from which you can see the water. The further you are willing to hike, the less likely the water has been fished by anyone else in the recent past. And the water is absolutely beautiful.

Take Hwy. 299 east from Redding about 40 minutes if you wish to fish the running water section of the Pit River arm of Shasta Lake. Turn left on Fenders Ferry Road and go another 20 minutes to where the road crosses high above the water. This is not couch potato fishing. Past the bridge you can park at one of numerous turnouts and scramble down the long, steep hill to the water. Because this fishing is so remote and clearly only for

the best physical specimens, the water gets very little fishing pressure. Look for rattlesnakes and poison oak on the hill, bring plenty of water with you, and never fish this section alone.

One more thing. The water on the Pit arm of Shasta Lake is subject to daily fluctuation from the Pit 7 Powerhouse upstream. Just be aware that depth and velocity of this running water might increase, wade accordingly. By all means pay attention. Don't waste time fishing the slower water and pools in this area since they contain few trout and many rough fish species. The trout are in the riffles and faster runs in this section.

THE LOWER SACRAMENTO

The flows below Keswick Dam through the city of Redding seem to have an inverse relationship to levels in Shasta Lake and create two very different rivers. In between Shasta Lake and Keswick Dam is nine miles of water called Keswick Reservoir that fluctuates not seasonally, but daily, and this unique fishery will be addressed separately in another section.

Located about three miles north of the city of Redding, the water referred to as the Lower Sacramento River emerges cold and deep from below Keswick Dam. For about 25 miles this river is considered one of the finest wild rainbow trout fisheries on the west coast, flowing right through the city of Redding, a growing city of almost 80,000 people.

From May through September is high water and the best access is via driftboat. Flows routinely range from 12,000 to 14,000 cfs making wading certain areas a foolhardy proposi-

◆

ACID Dam in Redding backs up water below Keswick Dam for agricultural use in the Sacramento Valley.

View of Mount Shasta from Castle Crags. Different groups believe the mountain possesses unique powers.

◆

long in the Sacramento River system, one thing remains constant. The successful angler has to think about how the changing flows might effect the fish, as well as access for fishing. A little knowledge and related strategic planning can produce impressive results.

OF SHAMANS, SUNKEN TREASURES AND THE MIGHTY HERCULES

It's true. There are enough intriguing facts about the Sacramento River system and surrounding lands to fill a book in its own right. But never forget that we are talking about a place called California, so you can bet the region also has more than its share of myths, legends, superstitions and interesting people who add a splash of color to an already vivid landscape.

The headwaters of the Sacramento begin within sight of majestic Mount Shasta towering over 14,000 feet above sea level. This, the second tallest peak in the lower 48 states, and the lushly forested hills and valleys surrounding have captured people's imaginations and spawned stories that, well, might sound a bit outrageous.

FROM THE LAND OF MU

First, there are the "Lemurians" who are widely held to inhabit subterranean tunnels and chambers in the area. What, you might well ask, is a Lemurian? None other than descendants of the lost continent of Mu, most of which was thought

◆

Joe Kimsey, owner of the Ted Fay Fly Shop in Dunsmuir, is known for promoting the use of traditional flies and angling techniques on the upper Sac.

tion. Most of the wading during high water months occurs in areas left high and dry during the low water months of October through April. High water puts the river level five to six feet higher than winter low flows, with a corresponding increase in velocity. This is big water that ought to be approached with a certain respect.

Usually around October flows are cut back once again causing Shasta Lake above to start gradually filling while creating numerous wading opportunities not available during high water. For the wading angler, winter is the season of almost unlimited access to the river and several peak seasonal fishing periods that have become well known among local anglers. Winter flows, barring unprecedented winter storms, average 4,000 to 5,000 cfs, and in many ways its like a different river.

It's obvious that trout would move around within the river as various hatches and other food sources become available through the year. But the huge fluctuation in water levels between the seasons intensifies this movement to the point where you cannot always count on water that's proven productive in the summer, producing well during the winter. In fact, that productive riffle you discovered last summer might not even be under water in the winter.

While it might seem that nothing stays the same for very

to have been plunged to the bottom of the ocean in the same cataclysm that sunk the lost continent of Atlantis.

There are thousands of intelligent, presumably sober individuals who are convinced the region around Mount Shasta and the headwaters of the Sacramento are all that's left of this once-great continent. This very advanced civilization miles underground as a hedge against future natural disasters. Lemurians have allegedly been sighted by many area residents, and even a few fishermen. They are reported to be tall with oversized bald heads and wear long white flowing robes. Almost any long-time resident of the area has encountered folks who claim to have met Lemurians, and a few will admit to it themselves.

The region also has a wealth of seemingly normal, everyday people who claim to have encountered such creatures as gnomes, fairies, or perhaps Bigfoot himself in the wilds that nest the headwaters of the Sacramento. When Mount Shasta so frequently catches easterly-moving clouds that shroud it's peak in shadow, some believe these clouds actually hide visiting extraterrestrial spaceships that are, perhaps, visiting the Lemurians. One member of the New Age Movement mentioned to me that Mount Shasta is considered to be a powerful conductor of psychic energy. However these stories got started, the area has a lot to offer if your run-of-the-mill fish stories ever become too mundane.

Perhaps some of these stories are a natural extension of the myths and legends passed from generation to generation by the Native Americans that inhabited this region for at least the last several thousand years. In fact, they are sitting on a solid foundation of local myths and legends that started with the first inhabitants (not Lemurians) of the region.

THE WINTU PEOPLE

Olelbis, Creator Spirit of the Wintu people, reached up and broke off a strip of the sky. Then, sharpening one end, plunged it into the earth at the base of Mount Shasta and carved out the McCloud and the Pit Rivers, and finally the Sacramento.

These Indians are known to have inhabited the Sacramento River drainage for at least 4,000 and perhaps as many as 10,000 years before the first white men appeared on the scene. First called Bohema-mem (Great water) by the Wintus, the river eventually came to be known as the Sacramento, the Spanish name for 'Holy Sacrament,' during Mexican occupation of the early 19th century.

According to Wintu legend, all life sprung from their beloved river and each man, women, tree, animal and fish was to be revered and respected as a connected part of their Creator. Perhaps the colorful people and lurid legends surrounding the river first set the stage for the remarkable romance people seem to feel for the Sacramento.

◆

Traditional upper Sac flies, some created by Ted Towendolly, some by Ted Fay, and others by Joe Kimsey.

Mike Mercer, retail manager of The Fly Shop in Redding hoists a pudgy lower Sac rainbow.

◆

The Wintus were very spiritual people who fancied every part of nature as having deep mystical significance in their lives. They believed in spirits as well as terrible giants called Supchets, (perhaps an early version of the Bigfoot legend?). While the culture relied heavily on the year-round runs of salmon and steelhead that gorged the river as a food source, each Wintu had deep respect for the life of each fish that was forfeit to sustain his own. Nothing was ever wasted. It's only speculation to suppose the Wintu's intimacy with the river contributed in any way to the success of the first and most famous fly fishing guide on the upper Sacramento River.

THE BEGINNING OF A TRADITION

Ted Towendolly, a Wintu man, established a fly fishing tradition in the area beginning in the 1920s. Through his work as a fishing guide, his methods and several of his original fly patterns are still being used on the river to this day, and they lend a special uniqueness to the river and fishing experience. Ted Towendolly eventually passed his flies and fishing technique along to Ted Fay, who became a legend along the upper Sacramento and established the Ted Fay Fly shop in Dunsmuir. After generations of guiding and fishing the river, Ted Fay

passed along these hard-won secrets to Joe Kimsey, the Ted Fay Fly Shop's present owner.

In those days, the 1920s, the Indian Way meant simplicity, practicality and results. The purpose of fishing was to catch fish, usually for the table and less frequently for sport. This is the attitude that gave way to a particular nymph fishing technique that developed along the upper Sac and has since spread far and wide over the entire fly fishing world. Most folks know it as "short line nymphing."

Ted's revolutionary technique went something like this, as described by Joe Kimsey: "You always fish two weighted flies. These are not nymphs, but weighted flies. You smack them down into the water upstream from a rock with no more than a couple of feet of fly line beyond the tip of your rod. Keep your rod low to the water and watch for twitches in the line, hesitations, maybe a slight change in direction and then, WHAM, cross his eyes!"

And things haven't changed very much in the way most people fish the upper Sac. After Ted Towendolly's death Ted Fay added to the compliment of original upper Sacramento River flies. But there was apparently no need to alter the technique which both Teds found so effective. In taking over the business from Ted Fay, Kimsey also added a few favorite fly patterns of

13

his own to the collection, but did not sway from the original fishing method. "Hell," said Kimsey, "why fix it if it ain't broke?"

THE LAST SHAMAN

Though historical records are a bit sketchy, Ted Towendolly was apparently kin to a man named Grant Towendolly (many believe he was his son), the last bona-fide Wintu Indian Shaman or medicine man. Those who witnessed Ted's talent for catching trout with his beloved Heddon Black Beauty bamboo fly rod probably suspected there was a touch of Indian magic involved.

In the Wintu culture the Shaman was the keeper of many things. In addition to having a vast knowledge of medicinal plants for treating numerous ailments, he (sorry, no women allowed) was responsible for passing down all the religious rituals and traditions of the tribe. These were not written by the Wintus, but rather were passed down from father to son in an oral tradition by rote memory.

With the advent of white settlers in the world of the Wintu, the tribe eventually became greatly dissipated and tribal unity was lost. But before his death in 1963, Grant Towendolly passed along his Wintu legends to Marcelle Masson, who recorded them in her book titled A Bag of Bones. By the vivid descriptions of spirits, giants and animals taking on human qualities passed along from the Shaman himself, Ted Towendolly the fishing guide undoubtedly grew up in a world full of wonder.

Unlike today, catch and release fishing was unheard of in those days. Instead of the wispy fly rods employed by Ted Towendolly, the weapon of choice for most of his kinsmen was a 14-foot long duel-tipped spear. But then again, there wasn't much sport involved in going hungry. Although salmon was the primary food source, the native rainbow trout of the river were approached by most Indians in a somewhat different fashion.

Hooks were fashioned from a particular bone found in the head of a deer and twine was made from the sinewy skins of streamside plants. Trout were in the habit of stationing themselves behind salmon redds in hope of intercepting dislodged eggs. The favorite bait was, you guessed it, salmon eggs. So if Ted Towendolly wasn't considered too much of an iconoclast for fishing for trout instead of salmon, he was certainly viewed as an "oddball" by his people for going after these fish with his fake bugs. And the thing about it was, he was exceedingly good at catching trout this way.

When railroad construction crews invaded the Sacramento River canyon in the 1880s the workers, like the native peoples, turned to the river for food. When you had a crew of hungry laborers to feed, there was nothing "unsporting" whatsoever about tossing a stick of dynamite into the river and serving whatever floated up. In very short order the fishery began to show signs of weakening as salmon and steelhead runs declined. But like the frequent disasters the fishery has suffered in recent history, the Sacramento River fishery has always shown a remarkable ability to bounce back.

SUNKEN TREASURES

Called the "Keystone of the Central Valley Project," the Sacramento River was dammed in the early 1940s below its confluence with the McCloud and Pit Rivers to form one of the largest reservoirs in the west called Shasta Lake. But hundreds of feet below the surface of this huge impoundment can be found historical remnants of Indian villages as well as entire towns once inhabited by thousands of miners and their families. Like most of the areas around these great waters, humans have lived, loved and died here for centuries. Now, instead of the hustle and bustle of busy lives, there is only the quiet lapping of waves and the call of the osprey.

The Report of the Commissioners of Fisheries of California, 1874-5 called the Baird Fish Hatchery "The largest establishment in the world for the hatching of salmon eggs." First constructed in 1872 by Livingston Stone on what was then the McCloud River, now deep under Shasta Lake, this huge facility was built to help shore up the already depleted stocks of Atlantic salmon in East Coast waters. By the early 1880s, however, local stocks of salmon were already falling on hard times. It was accepted that damage to the system by blasting railroad crews were the chief cause of the declining fishery. Baird Hatchery was closed and re-opened several times over the years, but finally shut down permanently in 1935. Eventually the entire area was then inundated by the waters of Shasta Lake.

It was a man named Jeremiah Blizzard Campbell who was the real friend to future generations of trout fishers. Campbell owned a ranch about eight miles up the McCloud River from the Baird Hatchery, also now at the bottom of Shasta Lake. He was the first one to collect and ship eggs from a previously unknown gamefish called the rainbow trout.

As common as rainbow trout seem today given their worldwide distribution and popularity, it's hard to imagine that it wasn't always so. But rainbow trout are native to the coastal drainages of the North American Continent. Campbell found an enthusiastic and immediate market for his discovery.

As it turned out, salmon weren't the only species suffering under the industrialization of the eastern United States. As early as the 1870s the native eastern brook trout was in a state of decline. Rainbow trout were found to be beautiful, acrobatic and tenacious fighters, great table fare and would readily take a fly. Campbell shipped his eggs first to the East Coast where, by around 1887, they had established themselves so well that domestic demand took a nosedive. Campbell then discovered that it wasn't only Americans who loved trout in their waters. Before he got out of the hatchery business, he established self-sustaining populations of rainbow trout in such far-away places as New Zealand, Chile, Argentina and even Yugoslavia.

OTHER BURIED TREASURES

Many others clung to the river systems of this region for their livelihood. Some of the first white men were first lured to

Box Canyon Dam is the beginning of the serious trout fishing water on the upper Sac.

the area by a word often spoken with deep and abiding reverence: gold. And many found it here too. After most of the gold played out many stayed around with their families in pursuit of other commodities like copper, zinc and silver.

One entire town, Kennett, lays at the bottom of Shasta Lake. Located directly north of massive Shasta Dam under about 400 feet of water, this once-great mining town boasted a population of over 10,000 souls. In fact, Kennett was so productive that sulfur fumes belched from the town's five smelters finally managed to kill virtually all vegetation within a 15 mile radius. This, along with the decline of copper prices after World War I led to the decline of the town and the smelters were finally shut down after 1925. Although too deep for most divers, rumors persist about an elegant Kennett tavern at the bottom of Shasta Lake with a long and beautiful mahogany bar perfectly preserved in the icy depths.

The town of Delamar lays beneath the Squaw Creek arm of Shasta Lake which was supported by the adjacent Bully Hill smelter. Captain Delamar of Utah was the first to build a smelter capable of processing copper ore locally and the town was established to house his employees and their families. In its prime the mine and smelter employed 2,000 men, and the population of Delamar grew to two or three times that. The town finally folded due to problems with zinc in the copper ore and lawsuits over damage to local vegetation from sulfur fumes. Today the ruins of the smelter can be seen just above the lake on the north side of the Squaw Creek arm. Interesting historic ruins highlight this part of the lake both above and beneath the surface of the water.

CAVE OF THE LOST MAIDEN

Also known as Samwel Cave, it can be found near the Ellery Creek campground on the McCloud arm of Shasta Lake. An ancient Wintu story persists about his place that is quite possibly more than just legend.

Long ago, as the story goes, three young Wintu girls consulted an old woman about where to go to find a man. The woman suggested this particular cave which was considered a "holy place" where men went in search of spiritual strength and bravery.

While making her way through the cave one of the girls supposedly slipped and fell down a deep shaft to her death. This story hung around for centuries and was well-known by most Wintus. Intrigued by the romantic tale, a team of University of California anthropologists made a trip to the cave in 1903. There they found the skeletal remains of an Indian girl at the bottom of a 75-foot deep pit within the cave. Sometimes fact is every bit as provocative as fiction.

THE MIGHTY HERCULES

Hercules was a large athletic man who lived out of the back of his station wagon and fished the Sacramento River frequently in the Redding area. Despite his unusual living arrangements, he was something of a mystery since he always looked

15

clean and well-kept. Although the Sacramento had been dammed by the early 1940s, there were still powerful runs of ocean fish and all "real men" fished for salmon. Hercules' real name has since faded into the mists of history, but Redding old timers still talk about the man celebrated as one of the most cunning fishermen in the area.

Hercules was not a fly fisher. No, he used ultralight spinning gear and fished behind the salmon redds for huge steelhead. Because his gear was so light, it always took him a long time to land his fish. He never waded like the other fishermen who were heaving great lures half-way across the river in hopes of snagging salmon. He made delicate 20-foot casts and hooked and played his fish with such artistry that he is remembered to this day.

Hercules was a kind of Paul Bunyun or Pecos Bill of the Sacramento, only real flesh and blood. Funny thing about fishermen; they never forget about their legends, fact or fiction. And like any good fish story, the truth is largely irrelevant.

One day Hercules just disappeared. Two or three years ago one old-timer thought he saw him adorned with a white beard gazing across the river in his old favorite spot. Perhaps Hercules was a wayward Lemurian?

◆

Called Klamath weed, delicate petals lend a shock of color to rocky upper Sac shorelines.

THE UPPER UPPER: BOX CANYON TO CASTLE CRAGS

I know a pool in a leafy dell that the wary trout love best and a timid trail to the chaparral where the red deer lays at rest a nightbird calls when the shadows fall and a cougar's lonely cry a silent deep and a dreamless sleep under the open sky.

From *A Siskiyou Memory* by W.P. Burns

The upper Sacramento River is celebrated as one of the most beloved and productive trout streams in America, and with good reason.

First, the upper Sac comes close to having everything. You name it. You can fish small stream water in a majestic canyon chiseled out of sheer granite rock; wide, open flats where the sky seems endless; or right through the middle of a town if you choose with kids playing baseball amid family picnics. There are productive shallows, bounteous deeps and fertile riffles; all with staggeringly clear water and many thousands of fish. Add to this a rich history and established fly fishing tradition that only adds to the ambience.

By way of definitions, the water above Shasta Lake is known as the upper Sacramento, and below Keswick Reservoir as the lower Sac. The focus of this section is the upper, upper Sacramento River, trout water that's become dear to generations of ardent anglers.

Although the headwaters of the upper Sac really begin in several tiny forks above Lake Siskiyou outside of the town of Mount Shasta, the classic trout water begins at Box Canyon Dam where it flows out from below. It is a rugged and imposing gorge rich in natural beauty. The water here is small, but there are plenty of deep pools providing holding water for big wild trout. The best access is off Ney Springs Road where there is parking close to the stream. You can either hike up or down and find plenty of good water.

The canyon is most popular in the spring when high water downstream makes wading a challenging proposition. Box Canyon is one of those places that's difficult to fish, if only because the scenery is so ruggedly beautiful. There are times you may need to just give in to it and sit down on a rock to drink it all in. Worse things could happen.

The entomology of the upper Sac is rich in mayflies, caddisflies, stoneflies and midges so it's often more important to get a drag-free drift than to be fishing a certain, specific fly pattern. The fish in this section are all wild rainbows and, as such, are not easily duped. The water is crystal clear so your best bet for both nymph and dry fly fishing is a 6X tippet and leader of at least 9 feet in length.

Springtime on the upper Sac means stoneflies and there are plenty of them in Box Canyon. Almost any golden stonefly nymph imitation in a #10-12 will produce fish if presented properly. Since the water is small there isn't much casting involved. A good choice is to follow the traditional method of short line nymphing as developed by the late-great Ted

California Department of Fish & Game sponsored a poster contest designed to give area school kids a sense of stewardship in the recovering upper Sac.

◆

Towendolly. What worked on this river in the 1920s is still exceedingly effective today. Just drive your weighted fly down behind a rock on a short line and watch for the slightest twitch or hesitation in the end of your line. Then, "cross his eyes!"

Another early season canyon favorite is fishing attractor dry flies in the pocket water, especially in the evenings. Just pop a bushy dry fly around boulders and get ready for some quick action. The trout probably take these to be stoneflies, but since no one has ever discussed this with the fish, it's up for grabs.

As the season progresses the canyon becomes less popular because it heats up and there isn't much shade. But by this time water levels downstream allow much greater wading access to lower reaches.

Below Box Canyon and Ney Springs, the river continues through more canyon before opening up above the Cantara Loop. Still relatively small water, Cantara (the site of the notorious 1991 Cantara toxic spill) is a popular access for its easy wading and numerous fish. Access is from the east side of the river off Azalea and Cantara Roads to a parking area along the river. Although small, the water here begins to reflect the riffle-run-pool, riffle-run-pool pattern that will continue downstream all the way to Shasta Lake.

After the golden stones have peaked early in the season, the next major hatch on the upper Sac is the *Epeorus* mayflies, often confused with the eastern March Browns. This is a larger mayfly so good imitations include the brown Bird's Nest nymph in a size #10 or an Adams dry fly in a #12. While these bigger bugs are hatching you can do well with dry flies even though

you may see no rising fish at all. Simply smack your dry fly down on the water around boulders, and hang on. The fish are incredibly quick so expect to miss or break off a number of them. This type of fishing doesn't leave much time for boredom.

As the season continues to warm, caddisflies play an ever-increasing role in the trout's diet. Pick up almost any rock from the river bottom and you will see countless brownish-green tubes containing *Brachycentrus* caddis worms. These tend to hatch April-May on the river and can make for some exciting sport. The other caddis worms you will see wiggling in the cracks and crevices of the rock are likely *Hydropsyche* caddis which spin webs instead of building tubes. These will hatch sporadically throughout the rest of the summer and into the fall season. You can match the hatch on either caddis by using the ubiquitous LaFontaine Sparkle Pupa nymphs in #10-12 in brown or olive. The only other fly you will need is the legendary Elk Hair Caddis in #12-14.

Moving downriver from the Cantara section, the next popular spot is Mossbrae Falls where a spring spills into the river over high, smooth rocks creating a waterfall as breathtaking as it is delicate. The pool below the falls can hold good fish in the deepest section tight up against the rock wall, especially in the spring of the year. Access is from Scarlett Way bridge where you can drive across the river and park. The hike up the railroad tracks takes from 20 to 40 minutes, depending on your physical condition. If you're willing to wade across the river you can park at the Prospect Street fishing access and cut the hike in half.

Prospect Street on the north end of the old railroad town of Dunsmuir has its own fishing access parking area. The water just above holds an immense pod of trout that prefer either the

◆

Perennial sweet peas are native to Europe, but are common along the upper Sac in areas where pioneer families settled.

Trout LIMIT

ZERO
(release all trout at once)

Artificial lures only
Barbless hooks only

1 Box Canyon Dam to Scarlett Way (in N. Dunsmuir)
2 Mouth of Soda Creek to Shasta Lake
3 All upper Sacramento R. tributaries

Last Saturday in April to November 15
Protect our recovering river! Report violators to CalTIP 1-800-952-5400

Above and below the town of Dunsmuir, special angling regulations protect stocks of wild native fish.

deep runs or the shadowy areas. Don't overlook the shaded areas underneath the numerous Indian Rhubarb (Elephant Ears) plants that hang seductively above the river. I chased about 40 trout out of one such area after my friend Garth swore it contained no fish. Remember, trout don't have eyelids! These upper Sac fish just love the shade.

Scarlett Way is the next access down and one of the few in this section where the angler can park on the west side of the river. Although there is much good pocket water in this area, don't overlook the deep pool downstream where a large rock (Elephant Rock) protrudes from the middle. Big trout seem to feel more secure in this deeper stretch and it can be one of the more consistent areas, particularly during hot summer months. There is an enticing cave behind the boulder on the east side of the river.

Dunsmuir City Park offers some of the best fishing in the area, even though the river flows right through the middle of town. Located off Dunsmuir Avenue, it features easy access, lots of fish, picnic tables and swing sets within a stones' throw of the stream.

Stagecoach Avenue off Dunsmuir Avenue will take you to the next downstream access below the I-5 Bridge. Just below the bridge with massive I-5 towering overhead is a short, deep pool containing many trout. You will need to use a floating strike indicator about eight feet above your nymph with several medium-sized split shot fixed one foot above the fly. Choice of fly is less important than how you present it. The bend pool just below also contains many fish, but it gets significant fishing pressure and should be considered only as a last resort.

From the I-5 Bridge downstream through the town of Dunsmuir is a fairly urban stretch of river with many houses and private property. While the fish are here, there are far more scenic areas downstream providing for a much more enjoyable angling experience. Take for example, Castle Crags.

The Spanish first called it Casa del Diablo (Abode of the Devil) and was the name given spectacular rock formations towering over the Sacramento River on the west side. Known today as Castle Crags, these lovely peaks stick up into the sky like so many jagged wolf teeth swiping at the air. From the south end of Dunsmuir on down, Castle Crags can be seen from various river locations for miles. With views of the Crags to the west and towering Mount Shasta (14,162 ft.) to the north, it can be said with some authority that anglers along the upper Sac often have their heads in the clouds.

Several late-season hatches are worthy of mention. First is the big *Isonychia* mayfly which begins hatching in significant numbers just after Labor Day. These are curious insects in that they are vigorous swimmers powerful enough to paddle upstream in slower water. What's significant about this is the trout key in on the motion of the bugs. They hatch and lay their eggs under cover of darkness, so it's rare to see them flying. But the nymphs are active throughout the day, especially in the

Shasta Retreat is an assemblage of cabins and year-round homes along the upper Sac in north Dunsmuir. Scarlett Way is the main artery through the settlement and the bridge marks the southern boundary of the wild trout section.

Spectacular Castle Crags are visible from much of the upper Sac below Dunsmuir.

afternoon. You can swing or twitch big, dark nymphs on a tight line and feel trout slash at it underwater.

The last big hatch of the season is the October Caddis (*Dicosmoecus*). These giant, moth-like creatures fill the air over the stream just before dark creating a spectacle of memorable proportions. Like huge snowflakes they dance above the water catching the last bit of fading sunlight as they lay their eggs. They tend to hatch in the tailouts of pools and nymphs or emerger patterns can do well here. It's also great fun to smack a big, clumsy Stimulator dry fly down around rocks in the evenings and watch the trout explode in an effort to get it. Life could be worse.

THE LOWER UPPER: CRAGS TO SHASTA LAKE

The lower stretches of the upper Sac reflect the diversity of this great river by becoming a much larger stream and offering other notable species of fish to pursue. Within this area the river goes through it's narrowest and broadest sections, both offering some pretty terrific and remote fishing possibilities.

Continuing downstream is Castle Crags State Park and Castella with the lovely tributary Castle Creek merging with the river in between. This is a popular area due to its proximity to several campgrounds. Most of this section is shallow with impressive numbers of mostly smaller fish. It is a place to go if

the size of fish isn't too important but you want easy fishing in spectacular surroundings. But then again, easy is a relative term when speaking of wild trout.

Sweetbriar is a small settlement of homes in a lushly shaded section of river offering consistent fishing along the seams and drop-offs. There is easy access within walking distance of the parking area on the west side of the railroad tracks. It is a

Sam's Market at Castella on the upper Sac is a landmark dating back to less hectic times.

19

A streamside spring at Castella testifies to an area known for pure water.

♦

particularly good bet on hot, sunny days when the trout would just as soon steal your polarized sunglasses.

The next area is Conant and it can offer some good fishing in a setting where you are less likely to run into other people. With the exception of the campground at Sims downstream, the stretch between Conant and Gibson is the most remote. But expect to pay a price for solitude.

Access to the remote sections of the upper Sac requires a willingness to walk and wade aggressively. When you plan to get off the beaten track it's not a bad idea to bring along a friend. The worst potential hazards include the ubiquitous rattlesnakes and poison oak. But it's easy to "get in over your head" while wading too.

Conant is a relatively shallow, brushy area and access isn't necessarily easy. Take care and bring along a wading staff and plenty of drinking water.

Flume Creek is a fairly unique section of river containing two of my favorite sections of the upper Sac. Park just off the freeway exit and scramble down through the blackberry vines and poison oak to the railroad tracks. Hike downstream past the confluence with Flume Creek and you will come to the narrowest section of the entire river. Up above there are sections where the river is 40 to 50 feet broad. But in this one spot the river passes through a low gorge containing the whole stream into about six feet across. It's anyone's guess how deep this little place is, but it opens up into a wide, deep pool where trout love to hit anything that comes out of the gorge.

The other spot is just upstream from where the path hits the railroad tracks. There is a bend pool, shallow riffle above, slower and deeper water below. Almost every evening of the season there's some sort of hatch going on here and the trout love to feast on the surface. There are only one or two places to stand in order to avoid tangling in the brush with your backcasts, but it's worth the trouble. Bring a flashlight. All the paths look the same in the dark and a few end in the middle of nowhere.

The next good area downstream is called Sims, after one of the pioneer settlers in this area. There is a popular campground here, several bridges over the river and a huge, flat area where you can see the fish. And therein is the problem.

Known as "Sims Flat," it is only possible to take these fish if you are able to present a fly with the utmost finesse. The maddening thing is being able to see the fish so clearly and getting refusal after refusal. Don't get me wrong, these fish have to eat. It's just that most fly fishers lack the subtle skill necessary to do well here consistently. But because it is such a beautiful place, perhaps it is worth improving your skill level just to be here.

The next section downstream is known as Gibson, and is made up of short riffles and long, deep pools. Because of it's depth, wading is limited to small areas, usually at the heads or tails of pools. Most of the river is contained within huge bedrock boulders that you can easily stand on and fish. This is also where another fish species, bass, three different species in fact, becomes important. During the warmer months of summer largemouth, smallmouth and Alabama spotted bass move into many of the deeper pools and provide the angler with a few more options.

The best tactic for trout is to fish weighted nymphs under the chutes where riffles dump into deeper pools. Although the water along the surface is moving pretty swiftly, trout often hang in the slower water underneath waiting to grab something from overhead. A nymph with enough split shot about a foot above the fly can be driven down through the faster water to where the fish are. Keep your line as tight as possible without actually dragging your fly downstream and watch for the slightest hesitation in the end of your fly line. Floating strike indicators will only suspend your fly above the fish in this deep water, instead of allowing it to get in the fish's face. Set the hook on anything.

Eagle Roost Road off I-5 provides access to most of Gibson and the next section down called Pollard Flat. You can exit at Pollard Flat from I-5 and turn toward the river, which is east. Turn left at the stop sign and then take a quick right turn down the gravel road through the open green gate. This is public property and will put you on one of the most picturesque sections of the stream with numerous riffles, runs and deep, blue pools. You can walk either up or down along the railroad tracks and see remnants of old mining cabins and much undisturbed water.

Try not to get caught crossing one of the several railroad bridges at Pollard Flat when a train comes through. Chances are good that you can plaster yourself far enough into the bridge railings to avoid being hit by the train, but who needs to worry about such things while fishing?

LaMoine is the next spot down and was the site of a prosperous lumber town at one time. Today there is nothing left but the old red house on the west side of the freeway to suggest

The riffle below Sims Campground is a popular and productive fishing area.

◆

there was ever anything there at all. Park at the top of the dirt road going down to the river unless you have a real 4-wheel-drive vehicle. Just past the railroad tracks is a marvelous deep pool with numerous trout and several species of bass.

Fish for the bass with full-sink or sink-tip fly lines and small, black leech patterns. They seem to especially go for an up-and-down jigging sort of motion of the fly. This is a great area for kids and families since on the other side of the pool is a series of boulders just tailor-made for diving or fishing. You can see big fish cruising the steep rocky ledges and all you need

◆

Looking down from the bridge at Sims, a merganser searches for lunch, or perhaps just a cool dip.

Smallmouth bass are an alluring alternative to warm-weather trout fishing.

Sandstone blocks carved by Chinese laborers over a century ago support this railroad bridge at Pollard Flat on the upper Sac.

do is drop your fly in front them. It's a great place to fish, swim, picnic or just spend time.

The lowest section of river just above Shasta Lake is known locally as McCardle Flat, but also encompasses Volmers and Dog Creek. This is the widest section of river with the most year-round flow. This section seems to have something for almost anyone and is very popular for its great trout and bass fishing. There are long, boulder-strewn riffles giving way to deep runs. Between Volmers and Dog Creek are several deep pools just made for bass fishing. Even though the water in this section tends to be warmer than upper sections, it contains many trout and many larger fish that migrate up from Shasta Lake. Take the Volmers Exit from I-5 and simply follow the signs to your choice of good fishing.

THE CANTARA INCIDENT:
SUDDEN DEATH AND REBIRTH OF A RIVER

About 9:50 p.m., July 14, 1991 I was having a hard time getting my young sons to go to sleep. Little did I suspect that just up the road from my home in Redding the upper Sacramento River was being executed by lethal injection; 19,000 gallons of metam sodium herbicide pouring forth death upon every fish, insect and plant in the stream. It would be many nights after that before I could manage a night's sleep without being haunted by imagined sounds of a million muffled fish screams.

It was a derailed Southern Pacific (SP) tanker car that had plunged from the bridge at Cantara—not the first time, but certainly the most lethal to this popular and beloved trout stream. This 97-car train was over a mile long, containing every commodity imaginable.

The so-called "Cantara Loop" is a notorious hairpin curve in the railroad tracks over the Sacramento River. Originally constructed in the 1880s, it was an engineering marvel in its day. Large crews of Chinese immigrants labored under the direction of rugged railroad men to finish what was to become the second tightest railroad loop in the country. What's more, the tracks climb 200 feet in one mile over a U-shaped curve offering an angler standing in the river the unusual sensation of being able to see a passing train coming and going at the same time.

It took the poison a little better than two days to bleed downriver 38 miles to Lakehead, the uppermost section of Shasta Lake. Reports came in hour-by-hour plotting the insidious downstream progress of this soil fumigant designed to kill, among other things, plants and insects. Thousands of concerned anglers were glued to radio and television reports in horror as they vividly witnessed the largest inland hazardous substance spill in California history. The state Department of Fish and Game immediately closed the entire area to fishing and, with the help of the California Highway Patrol, shut down access roads to the river as well as massive U.S. Interstate 5.

Desperate situations apparently require desperate actions, but for a time experts were perplexed about the best way to remove the toxin from the ecosystem. Then, less than a week after the spill a group of hazardous materials specialists were allowed to experiment with an innovative tech-

Approximately 235,000 trout, many of them trophies, quickly succumbed to the effects of the poison.

The so-called "Cantera Incident," dumped approximately 19,000 gallons of the herbicide metam sodium into the upper Sac killing all life down to Shasta Lake.

nique previously untried.

The strategy called for garden-variety air to be pumped into the lake underneath the front of the slowly encroaching poison. Mixing with air dissipated the substance and miraculously left non-toxic materials in its place. In short order the experiment was deemed a success and the emergency was over. But there was still a dead river to be cleaned, a recovery to be closely monitored as well as legal, economic and political questions to be answered. The real work was about to begin.

PICKING UP THE PIECES

As can be imagined, it took a while before the extent of the damage could be assessed and there was much confusion. The poison had coursed right through the middle of Dunsmuir, a small town several miles below Cantara. Residents soon complained of a variety of health conditions and were given medical attention at an emergency clinic set up in Dunsmuir High School.

Southern Pacific Transportation Company, owners of the railroad, went to work immediately to help the local community in numerous ways to minimize its expected losses. The massive transportation company made economic settlements with many businesses and private individuals whose health and/or economic well-being were effected by the spill. They retained

consultants to assess environmental and economic damage to the area, as well as to monitor every aspect of the river's recovery.

California's Department of Fish and Game went to work as well. Charged with ultimate responsibility for managing the river's recovery, they set their own team of scientists and consultants to work, at times almost competing with the SP team for position on the river. While scientists on both sides were delirious about the opportunity to examine the total reconstruction of an ecosystem from start to finish, the ominous shadow of high-stakes legal maneuvering loomed in the background. Everyone knew the price tag on the disaster was likely to be astronomical.

In addition to over a million dead fish (about 235,000 trout), aquatic insects, all manners of amphibian, plants, snails and mollusks were effected. Scientists collected thousands of specimens that were bagged and frozen for future study. Meanwhile, though the general strategy was to let the river recover as naturally as possible, certain projects were undertaken to either prevent further loss of life or help "jump start" various parts of the recovery process.

Forty-seven wild trout were captured from the two-mile stretch of river above the spill and brought to the Mount Shasta Fish Hatchery for spawning. The plan was to re-stock sections of the river with genetically native stocks of rainbow trout to

Rainbow Trout. Photo by Brad Jackson.

Garter snakes are common along most of northern California's waterways winding their way through streamside rocks and brush.

help get the fishery back a little quicker. The captured wild fish didn't take to the hatchery food or environment as scientists had hoped and many died. As a result only 7,000 fingerlings survived, far fewer than scientists hoped, to be re-seeded. A similar re-seeding program was accomplished for the native sculpin, the most abundant fish in the river. But for the most part the river was left pretty much alone to recover naturally, and the results were impressive.

Early after the spill business concerns feeling the loss of tourist dollars united with SP to petition for immediate re-stocking of hatchery trout in at least the tributaries of the upper Sac. After going back and forth several times, the idea was squelched as self-serving and not in the best interest of the river's recovery. But this was far from the last time this tune would be played. SP and others brought constant pressure to bare against the California Fish and Game Commission to re-stock the upper Sacramento River with hatchery fish as soon as possible.

LOOKING BACK

In order to fully understand the ramifications of re-stocking the river, a bit of history is in order. Prior to the spill at Cantara not much scientific information had ever been gathered on the upper Sacramento River fishery. Compared to some other parts of the United States, the known history of this area is relatively new. The first non-Native Americans to inhabit this region of northern California were Hudsons Bay trappers working through the area in the early 19th century. Before they arrived on the scene, an Indian culture thrived along these waterways which provided an almost unlimited source of food from abundant salmon and steelhead runs.

The railroad breached the Sacramento River canyon in the late 1880s providing transportation, employment and access to outside markets for local residents, and towns like Dunsmuir got a foothold in this rugged country. Fishing was immediately popular in Dunsmuir since the fabulous Sacramento River flowed right through the heart of town. Catch and release fishing hadn't even been considered in these days and probably wouldn't have made much sense to most people. Even before the railroad had taken its toll on the fishery, gold miners and timber barons had also taken their turns. What had previously been seen as an invincible fishery began to decline.

The first to suffer were the salmon and steelhead. Gold dredging through salmon redds, turning spawning tributaries into flumes that carried timber to mills and the continual blasting that created the railroad right-of-way were not conducive to a thriving fishery. But there was always trout, or so people thought. But Dunsmuir had continued to grow as the town became more important as a railroad stop and service center. The population grew because there was employment and it was a nice place to raise a family. Fishing "their" river became the favorite family pastime, and most folks fished worms and crickets for trout. Eventually the trout fishery also began to succumb to the fishing pressure, but a solution was close at hand.

California's first trout hatchery (and first west of the Mississippi) was built on Wagon Creek, a tributary of the upper Sac just up the road from Dunsmuir. Back in the 1930s little was known of the effects of planting hatchery fish on top of healthy wild strains and after all, trout were trout. It seemed the perfect solution to a beleaguered fishery, and what was the harm anyway? This signaled the beginning of an angling tradition that persists in the town of Dunsmuir to this day.

It was determined that by the spring of 1994 the river had recovered sufficiently to sustain some limited angling. Fish and Game Commission meetings in California had taken on aspects of "Clash of the Titans" as Southern Pacific attorneys squared off against conservation groups like California Trout, Federation of Fly Fishers and Trout Unlimited. SP wanted hatchery fish in the river as soon as possible; conservation groups generally wanted the river left to recover naturally with wild fish. The uneasy compromise called for hatchery fish and bait fishing in Dunsmuir; wild fish, artificials only and catch and release fishing everywhere else. California Trout even organized a massive litter pickup campaign during the summer of 1992 that removed over 100,000 pounds of trash from the river corridor.

REVELATIONS

Question: What was the greatest lesson learned from the Cantara Spill? Answer: How horribly the upper Sacramento Trout fishery had been taken for granted and mis-managed for generations. Studies have proven the old axiom "You never know what you've got until you lose it" applies to the upper Sacramento River, in spades.

Biologists usually rely on snorkel surveys and electrofishing to determine the density of fish populations in running water, neither method being especially accurate. But in the case of the upper Sac, biologists had the opportunity to count fish corpses. It doesn't get much more accurate than that. What they discovered was that the upper Sac had been a "sleeping giant" among trout fisheries, with wild fish populations on a par with any blue ribbon trout fishery in the nation.

Joe Kimsey (left) and Ron Rabun are both experienced upper Sac fishing guides.

In addition to the untold millions of hatchery fish stocked in the river since the 1930s, biologists discovered the upper Sac also sustained 7,000 to 8,000 wild rainbow trout per mile. Even at the time of the spill, the height of stocking season, hatchery fish represented less than 15 percent of the dead fish counted. This could perhaps put future management of the river in a different light since, instead of the put and take fishery the river had been considered to be, the river's true identity as a premier wild trout stream has now been revealed.

In an effort to learn more about angling patterns along the river, Department of Fish and Game initiated a creel census in 1994. In Dunsmuir, as might be expected, 51 percent of the anglers fished with bait, 34 percent flies and 14 percent lures. Fly fishers lead the pack with a catch rate averaging .82 fish per hour. Bait anglers caught .75 fish per hour and lure fishermen .66 fish per hour. Unofficial reports suggest that about seven out of ten fish caught on flies in the Dunsmuir area are wild fish. Outside of the Dunsmuir area 82 percent of all anglers on the stream were fly fishers, 16 percent used lures and 2 percent ignored angling regulations and used bait.

THE FUTURE

You might think after Southern Pacific agreed to an out-of-court settlement of $38 million and happy anglers returned to the river to terrific fishing all would be forgotten. Not so. Nothing in California ever happens that easily. Management of the upper Sacramento trout fishery promises to remain a political football for years to come. On one side are the Dunsmuir old-timers, and business development types versus the conservation groups and fly fishing organizations—the former scream-

Renowned fly tier Andy Burk showcases a few of his Shasta Lake patterns, showing that creating just the right fly for Shasta Lake trout and bass can be as much fun as the fishing

ing to return the river to management of the past (liberal stocking of hatchery fish throughout the river and bait fishing), while the latter prefers wild trout and restrictive angling regulations. How will things turn out? Well, as they say way down in Hollywood, "stay tuned."

THAT BIG PUDDLE IN THE MIDDLE: A FLY FISHER'S GUIDE TO SHASTA LAKE

They said it couldn't be done. For years it was considered absurd to try to fish massive Shasta Lake with a fly rod. The water was too big, too deep and more rightly the province of the Budweiser Pro Bass Fishing Team. They were wrong.

Shasta Lake was created back in 1943 when a dam was completed to catch the combined flows of the Sacramento, McCloud and Pit Rivers. Called the "Keystone of the Central Valley Project," it was conceived to provide cheap hydro-electric power to a growing western population as well as to gain control over unpredictable water conditions for agriculture. It boasts 270 miles of shoreline and depths in some areas over 400 feet.

In addition to the native trout trapped behind the gargantuan structure, non-native fish species were also introduced to maximize the sport fishery. Over the years many experiments failed as various species couldn't adapt to Shasta, but several have been successful enough to create the immensely popular fishery we have today. But it has to be approached on its own terms. If you want the best fishing, you have to have the right equipment.

By far the best way to access this big water is from a power boat. Unless you plan to limit yourself to fishing one specific small area (a less than brilliant idea on Shasta), leave your float tube and tiny pram at home. Part of the appeal of Shasta is its beauty and openness. Plan to see some of it while you hunt for fish. The other necessary piece of equipment is an electronic fish-finder.

I know there are a few "purists" out there eager to pooh-pooh the use of such technology in fly fishing. Well, let them waste all their time going nowhere and fishing blind on Shasta while the rest of us catch fish. Leave it at that. There's simply too much water here to approach it any other way. A power boat will allow you to get around Shasta efficiently and the fish-

With the habits of a smallmouth and the size of a largemouth, this Alabama spotted bass has become a much-pursued prize on Shasta Lake.

finder will tell you where the fish are. Remember, you still have to get them to bite.

Shasta is about both trout and bass. It was discovered they could easily co-exist since the bass generally prefer warmer water than trout. Successful fly fishing means learning to "surf the thermocline." The expression refers to the stratification of water in a lake by temperature.

In summer the warmer water is on top, so most fishing is for bass. During the winter the opposite is true with both the cold water and trout up near the surface. In reality, even with modern sinking lines, the deepest a fly fisher can effectively fish is about 20 feet. Nevertheless, this is enough to put terrific numbers of bass and trout within reach of the fly angler at various times of the year, and sometimes both species in the spring and fall as the lake "turns over."

SPRING AND SUMMER

The problem with April is it offers too many choices. In the back of my mind is the knowledge that the Brachycentrus caddis hatch on the lower Sacramento in Redding is at its peak. There can also be some terrific opportunities to fish the same hatch for truly monster trout on upper Keswick Reservoir. But the lure of Shasta Lake is often strong enough to drag me away from these other great fishing locations. Shasta has its own brand of appeal and offers several exciting choices of its own.

The first is bass. Shasta contains three species of bass, all worthy adversaries on a fly rod. There are largemouth, smallmouth and Alabama spotted bass to pursue, each having their own habits and preferences. Largemouth tend to be the largest and prefer warmer water. The smallmouth bass are smaller and like cooler water, rocky points and walls. Alabama spotted bass (known locally as "spots"), grow as big as largemouth but have the same habits as smallmouth bass. They have become the most abundant bass species in Shasta and are immensely popular with anglers.

April is an excellent time to fish for bass because they are in a spawning frame of mind. In other words, they're in shallow water and very aggressive. But a brief explanation of each species and how they adapt to Shasta is in order. All three species can be found everywhere on Shasta Lake so, like fishing in the ocean, you're never quite sure what you're going to come up with. Nevertheless, a bit of background will improve your chances with each specific target species.

Largemouth bass prefer warmer water than either smallmouths or spotted bass. Of the various arms of Shasta Lake, largemouth seem to generally prefer the Pit arm for its warmer water and abundant cover. Before Shasta Dam was completed huge crews of loggers methodically stripped most of the timber from areas about to be inundated with water. But then World

Like witch's fingers groping for the sky, snags on the Pit River arm of Shasta Lake provide excellent bass habitat.

Shasta Dam is the "plug" in the system creating Shasta Lake, one of the largest reservoirs in the west.

War II broke out and the boys were called overseas before the Pit arm of Shasta Lake could be harvested. Today, over 50 years later, you can still see areas of the Pit arm where twisted remnants of dead timber reach above the surface of the lake like dead fingers. But this is largemouth bass heaven.

Most of Shasta is deep and the banks are steep. There aren't a lot of shallow areas or the lilly-padded cover usually associated with warm-weather bass fishing. Your fish-finder will prove to you that bass often hang a foot or two off the bank and usually right on the bottom. Fish suspended in the water column tend to be trout on Shasta. Seek out shallow coves, brushy areas and snags to fish around if you want to catch largemouth bass.

Smallmouths and spots seem to prefer rocks over vegetation for cover. There are numerous areas of Shasta where rocky cliffs drop off into inky-deep water only a few feet from shore. It isn't uncommon to have your boat five or six feet off the bank while your fish-finder shows the water is over 100 feet deep. Thankfully you don't have to fish deeper than about 20 feet to do well. "Cove hopping" is often a very effective technique on Shasta. Most fishing is casting in toward the bank with sinking lines and leech or streamer patterns that imitate threadfin shad. Occasionally you can fish for bass with floating lines, but you will be severely limited.

A seven or eight weight rod is the weapon of choice for most bass fishing in this area, and the longer rods will handle more line. A Type III or IV uniform sinking line is a good choice but sink-tips will work almost as well. Shasta bass can sometimes be lured to the surface but aren't as willing to leave the bottom as bass in other lakes.

The best place to locate rainbow and brown trout during warmer months is far up the various arms where the cooler waters merge with Shasta Lake. Shasta trout may be either wild or hatchery fish, but few fish in this water are ever small. An initial stocking of about 200,000, 10 or 11-inch rainbows are planted in the spring with regular plants continuing throughout most of the summer. Because of the abundance of threadfin shad in the lake, it takes only a few months for these hatchery trout to reach 16 inches or larger. Most of the trout caught exceed 18 inches. There are also plenty of wild rainbow and brown trout in Shasta.

FALL AND WINTER

During cooler months most fly anglers go after Shasta Lake trout. While the major tributaries like the Sacramento, McCloud and Pit rivers close to fishing around November 15th, Shasta Lake is open all year. As long as you are fishing below the last riffle in these running water systems, it is legally considered part of the lake. In other words you can find some high-quality stream-like fishing for big trout in these areas even after the traditional trout season has ended. Besides, its one of the best times of the year to be on Shasta.

Picture sparkling clear, slowly-moving water much like a

Ironically known as Spring Creek, this stream acts as a conveyor for toxic heavy metals from Iron Mountain Mine into Keswick Reservoir.

classic spring creek. Add to this clear blue skies, dense forests and rocky cliffs all around you underneath the occasional passing bald eagle. Now realize its February, you're wearing a T-shirt and there's no one else around. But don't get too wrapped up in the novelty of the situation or you'll miss the hatch.

Mayflies, caddisflies and midges ride the currents from the rivers into Shasta's slower water and the fish, especially in the evenings, line up to get them. This is more like traditional trout fishing with floating lines and nymphs under strike indicators or dry flies. You can anchor your boat and fish or park your boat and walk the banks. There are terrific opportunities to catch winter trout in the Sacramento, McCloud and Squaw Creek arms of Shasta all winter long.

The important thing is not to be intimidated by Shasta's huge size. Look at it this way: With a little strategic planning and the right equipment, Shasta Lake offers a variety of high quality fly fishing experiences for bass and trout. All you have to do is decide what kind of fishing you want to enjoy each day, and go for it.

FISHING THE FAR SIDE OF THE MOON

ON KESWICK RESERVOIR,
THE NORMAL RULES DON'T APPLY

Below Shasta Dam there's a mysterious ribbon of trout water that defies traditional stillwater fishing methods. Stretching about nine miles before coming to the next dam in the system, Keswick Reservoir shares attributes of both lake

and stream and beckons to those who have learned to keep an open mind. Wild rainbow trout to 19 pounds provide sufficient motivation.

You would expect water shackled between two dams to provide angling that's safe, predictable and perhaps a little on the mundane side. Northern California is full of such afterbay fisheries that tend to attract a sedentary crowd of anglers. Not so with Keswick. This water is deep, narrow, and the current fast, especially toward the upper end. Water levels in this fishery fluctuate as much as 10 feet in a given day. Not for the faint of heart, Keswick Reservoir is tailor-made for the angler willing to take risks in exchange for the chance at a real trophy.

To fish Keswick properly, take most everything you ever learned about fly fishing for trout and toss it out the window.

♦

Spring Creek.

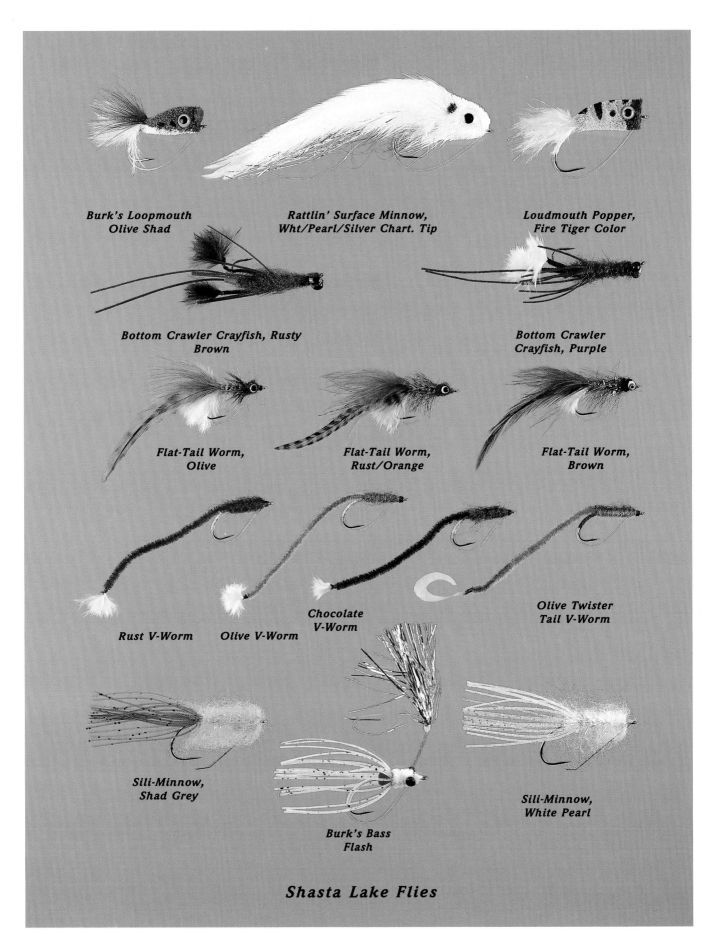

Burk's Loopmouth
Olive Shad

Rattlin' Surface Minnow,
Wht/Pearl/Silver Chart. Tip

Loudmouth Popper,
Fire Tiger Color

Bottom Crawler Crayfish, Rusty
Brown

Bottom Crawler
Crayfish, Purple

Flat-Tail Worm,
Olive

Flat-Tail Worm,
Rust/Orange

Flat-Tail Worm,
Brown

Rust V-Worm

Olive V-Worm

Chocolate
V-Worm

Olive Twister
Tail V-Worm

Sili-Minnow,
Shad Grey

Burk's Bass
Flash

Sili-Minnow,
White Pearl

Shasta Lake Flies

Burk's Yellow jacket

Burk's Spent Hopper

Silhouette Dun

Burk's CDC Lil' Yellow Stone Dry

Burk's Leg Nymph

Poxyback Pale Morning Dun Nymph

Poxyback Baetis Nymph

Poxyback Green Drake Nymph

HBI

Bead Thorax HBI

October Emerger

Sparkle Quill Pupa

Lt. Green Mercer's Z-Wing Pupa

Green Mercer's Z-Wing Pupa

Lt. Tan Mercer's Z-Wing Pupa

Tan Mercer's Z-Wing Pupa

Gold Bead Poxyquill Golden Stone

Poxy Back Golden Stone

Lil' Yellow Stone Nymph

Gold Bullethead

Silver Bullethead

Upper Sacramento River Flies

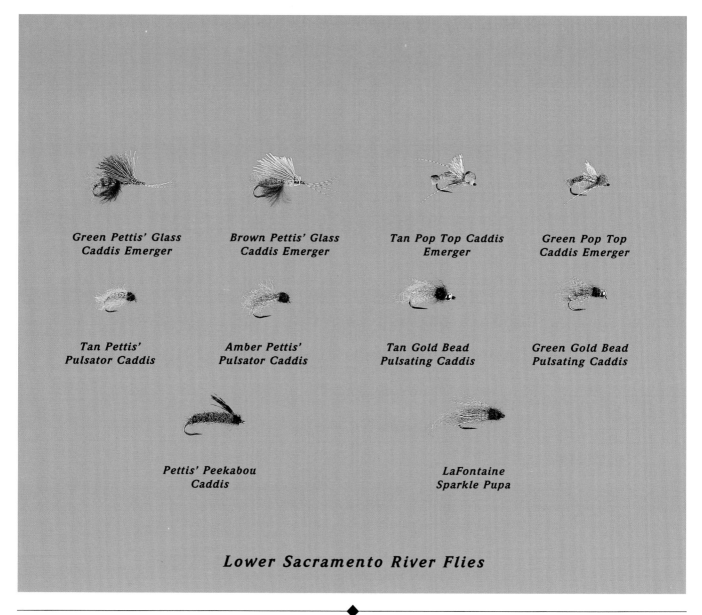

Green Pettis' Glass
Caddis Emerger

Brown Pettis' Glass
Caddis Emerger

Tan Pop Top Caddis
Emerger

Green Pop Top
Caddis Emerger

Tan Pettis'
Pulsator Caddis

Amber Pettis'
Pulsator Caddis

Tan Gold Bead
Pulsating Caddis

Green Gold Bead
Pulsating Caddis

Pettis' Peekabou
Caddis

LaFontaine
Sparkle Pupa

Lower Sacramento River Flies

◆

This is going to be a different sort of experience. Unbelievably, in all of Keswick's nine miles, there are very few places to wade or fish from shore. Access is limited by a brushy shoreline, deep water and, at times, a fast current. Leave your float tubes, prams and electric motors at home. Anglers experienced with Keswick agree the only efficient (and safe) way to fish it is from a power boat with at least a 10-horsepower motor.

Now the good news: Because access is limited, Keswick receives very little fishing pressure. The only ramp where you can launch a boat is located about one mile north of Keswick Dam on the west side of the reservoir off Iron Mountain Road. The drill goes something like this:

Launch in the morning and sacrifice the first half-hour for motoring up to the limits of navigation just below Shasta Dam. The closer you get to the gargantuan concrete structure the stronger the current becomes. Pay attention and always travel up and down the main channel. The edges harbor ominous bedrock outcroppings that rise above or dip below the surface depending on how much water is being released. As you travel upstream, you will notice that more than the abundant bird

life captures your attention.

Bring along both floating and sinking fly lines. In most cases you will be fishing the slower water between the main channel and the bank. While fishing, this is also where you want to anchor your boat.

Although the quarry is wild rainbow trout, successful Keswick anglers develop a kind of "Zen" attitude toward how they pursue their fish. The surprising truth is that tactics used in locating Keswick trout are a lot like fishing for bass. These trout can usually be found hanging off structure like big boulders, snags and drop-offs. If there are no trout rising (which is normally the case) plan to start fishing with a sinking line.

WARMER MONTHS

Keswick is open to fishing year-round. In warmer months a good opening gambit is to twitch a caddis pupa seductively through the likely-looking holding water. Vary your retrieve from slow to fast, then back to slow again. I'm not totally sure if Keswick is more like a lake that acts like a river or vise-versa.

No, they're not all huge, but any wild trout you catch in February is the proper antidote to cabin fever.

At any rate the angling is an entertaining mixture of the best of both lake and stream fishing. The caddis of the warmer months are exactly the same as the dominant insects found in the lower Sacramento downstream from Keswick Dam, principally the Brachycentrus and Hydropsychids.

Sometimes it becomes difficult to remember this water is both lake and stream; but in summer months you can fish sections of upper Keswick in much the same ways you fish the river below. That is, caddis pupa imitations under strike indicators until the hatch comes off, then caddis emerger patterns and dry flies after that. There are certain times when some truly huge trout will rise selectively, smashing the surface of the water in hot pursuit of these quickly-moving insects. And what's especially nice about Keswick is that these trout don't see nearly the numbers of anglers as either the water above or below.

Although Keswick has hatches of mayflies, caddisflies and midges throughout the year, in the normal absence of hatching insects your best bet is to fish sinking fly lines and patterns that either imitate leeches or threadfin shad. Don't waste good fishing time by lingering too long fishing the main channel of the lake, especially toward the upper end. The water there can be dangerous and not nearly as productive as slower eddies along the sides. It seems the fish don't want to fight the heavy current any more then anglers do.

THE WINTER FISHERY

In winter months the fly pattern I reach for first is the midge pupa, using the same slow-fast-slow twitch method with a sinking line. Look for the slower water around submerged boulders and experiment until you find the right depths and retrieves.

Strike indicators are something of a mixed blessing and I tend to shy away from them whenever possible. Nevertheless, you can't argue the fact that in circumstances where you have to cast long distances, like on Keswick, they allow an angler a much greater likelihood of detecting strikes. To some, chucking a fly out into still or slowly moving water and staring at a strike indicator might seem like "no-brainer" fishing, and an awful lot like fishing worms underneath a bobber. But Keswick trout can be spooky and I recommend getting cozy with the technique.

It seems that fishing streamer patterns that imitate threadfin shad work better during the cooler months. At times, like on Shasta Lake above, you will see great schools of these silvery creatures darting around just beneath the surface and occasionally flying clear of the water in attempts to escape big feeding trout. If you are lucky enough to witness such an event and to be within casting distance, you won't even need a sinking line. Just cast your streamer into the fray and hang on.

Western fence lizards sunbathe along the rocky banks of the lower Sac waiting for hapless insects to fly within range.

The average lower Sacramento River rainbow is over 16 inches, with many fish much larger.

WATCHING THE WATER

No matter what time of the year you are fishing Keswick Reservoir, pay close attention to the water levels. They change often and sometimes dramatically. Anglers experienced with Keswick always have tales to tell, occasionally with lurid descriptions of near-death experiences when the water either went up or down unexpectedly.

Once I listened breathlessly to a man describing an experience he had when the anchor of his boat got caught on the bottom as the flow was coming up. He had a short anchor rope that day. When the water started to come up he had no more slack line to pay out, raising the bow of his boat up in the air as it pulled the stern toward the bottom. In several desperate moments he was able to hack through the anchor rope in the nick of time to keep from going under.

The opposite scenario can be just as frustrating even if not as potentially dangerous. One local guide pulled his boat to shore to eat lunch around the corner under a shade tree. When he returned he found his boat high and dry and perched on a rocky shoal. In such cases you have little choice but to wait for the water to come back up again, however long that might take.

MYSTERY FISH

There is very little biological information available on the origins of the trout in Keswick Reservoir. Naturally there were native rainbow trout and probably a few steelhead trapped in the system when Keswick dam was completed. But the reservoir has been used in the past as a kind of "dumping ground" for surplus hatchery fish. Over the years rainbows, browns and kokanee salmon have found there way into Keswick from various area fish hatcheries. The last planting on record occurred over a decade ago, but scientists are somewhat confounded over exactly where Keswick's abundant fish life originates.

Several small tributaries toward the upper end of Keswick could potentially be used for spawning, but during the spring spawning season many of these are infused with high levels of heavy metals; dark remnants from the area's mining history. It's estimated there are at least 1,100 abandoned mines of various sizes in the vicinity; the runoff can damage water quality and harm aquatic life.

All we know for sure is the fish are here, and what more do we need? It's especially hard to imagine how this fishery flourishes considering what feeds into Keswick's lower end.

IRON MOUNTAIN MINE

Not far below the boat launch ramp on the west side of Keswick a small tributary with an ironic name feeds the system. Called Spring Creek, it is a vehicle carrying toxic heavy metal waste from the giant Superfund site called Iron Mountain Mine. Here is a classic example of mankind creating an envi-

Reviving lower Sac rainbow

◆

ronmental problem so complex that we haven't yet developed the technology to completely fix it.

The bowels of Iron Mountain Mine, just west of Keswick, have been referred to as the most acidic place on earth. This area has been heavily mined for over a century and there are empty chambers within the mountain that could fully contain a modest skyscraper. Until as recently as two years ago it dumped more than a ton of toxic heavy metals into the depths of Keswick Reservoir each day.

Finally a new treatment plant was constructed to neutralize about 70 percent of the mine's discharge. Runoff from the mine is worst in spring when heavy rainfall is most likely. In wet years heavy metal-laden water spills over the dam forcing flows in the system to increase dramatically. For every one part of runoff that enters the Sacramento River system via Keswick Reservoir, 30 to 40 parts of additional water are required to dilute it to avoid killing all streamborn life downstream, not to mention the fact that Redding relies heavily on the system for its drinking water. Spring Creek Debris Dam was erected as a catch basin to allow a controlled release into Keswick; it is scheduled to be doubled in size.

Although the treatment plant is helping, the process used produces a kind of sludge. Scientists estimate there is no end in sight to the production of this sludge and there has been hot controversy over exactly what to do with it.

Downstream from Spring Creek, Keswick's slow current keeps most of the toxic wastes toward the western side of the reservoir. Still, the bottom of this area is devoid of life and no one knows how to handle the untold tons of heavy metals. Even under these extreme circumstances the Keswick trout fishery seems to thrive. Keswick Reservoir is atypical as a trout fishery in nearly every respect and, perhaps just for that reason, attracts a devoted following of anglers. Perhaps this is your day to try something really different.

SPRING AND SUMMER ON THE LOWER SAC: CADDIS, CADDIS, CADDIS

Just think of it. A world-class wild trout stream where the average fish is over 16 inches flowing right through the middle of a city of 72,000 people. You can fish dry flies for impressive rainbows within easy sight of hundreds of people sitting at desks, working at their computers and talking on the telephone. The best part is, at least for today, you're not one of them.

Clearly, the answer to catching these magnificent fish most of the time is caddisflies. The entomology of the lower Sac is indeed rich, about 2500 insects per square foot of river bottom, and heavily tipped in favor of the caddis. Two bugs in particular, the *Brachycentrus* and *Hydropsychid* caddisflies, are super-abundant and carry the fish and the angler through most of the warmer months.

THE BLANKET CADDIS HATCH

When conditions are right—low water and warm, sunny weather—there is one hatch on the lower Sac that can be ranked right up there with salmonflies on the Madison. Called the "blanket caddis hatch" for the way the insects seem to carpet the surface of the river, the springtime *Brachycentrus* hatch is a world-class angling event. It's one of those legendary times when an angler can witness hundreds of fish rising with abandon to untold millions of insects. The challenge, of course, is getting the trout to choose your bug.

Beginning most years in March, you can tell the hatch has started by the green blotches you get on your windshield when crossing the river on any one of several bridges. If the river is anywhere between 3,000 and 6,000 cfs, you can be assured of numerous wading opportunities. Too much water in some years not only limits access, but seems to adversely effect the hatch as well.

◆

Like prospectors of old, modern anglers find a pot of gold at the end of every rainbow.

Guides Scott Saiki (left) and Art Teter taking advantage of a day off in downtown Redding.

◆

Begin the day fishing larger nymphs like #10 Birds Nests or Prince Nymphs under strike indicators and 4X tippets. Fix a fluffy yarn indicator about six feet up from your fly and use at least two medium-sized split shot about a foot up from your fly. As the day wears on you should switch to smaller flies like a #12 LaFontaine Sparkle Pupa or Mercer's Z-Wing Pupa. When the trout start rolling on the surface it's time to switch again to

emerger patterns and finally dry flies. At times the fish won't settle for anything but a perfect drift and 5X tippets.

The evening spinner fall can be outrageous. *Brachycentrus* caddisflies lay their eggs by diving under the surface of the water, so you can forget "dead drift." There are times when swinging an Elk Hair Caddis on the surface or a standard soft-hackle pattern under the surface will bring hits on just about every cast. A word of caution: Even when fishing heavier 4X tippets, expect to break off lots of fish.

Some of my fondest memories have been fishing various stages of this hatch for huge rising trout. Look for places that funnel the current concentrating the food and the trout will be there. Fishing dry flies for jumbo wild fish is a time to remember.

THE HYDRO HATCH

Lasting much longer than the blanket caddis, the Hydropsychid caddis hatch carries through most of the warmer months. This slightly larger, net building caddis proliferates in tailwater fisheries throughout the west.

Flows in the Sacramento are usually increased in May, when the blanket caddis begins to taper off. Almost as if to pick up the slack for bored fly fishers, the Hydro caddis steps in right about this timb with only a few differences in tactics and flies used in fishing the blanket caddis hatch.

For one thing, the *Brachycentrus* caddis is olive in color and imitations should reflect this general coloration. The Hydros are more of an amber brown color and usually one size larger than flies used to imitate *Brachycentrus*. And just like the blanket caddis, trout are suckers for dry flies skated on a tight line at dusk. You will see plenty of naturals on the water skittering a little wake behind them like tiny waterskiers. It drives the trout wild.

◆

Reviving a battle-weary lower Sac rainbow can mean all the difference to the survival of the fish.

Photo by Brad Jackson.

After spawning, giant king salmon contribute nutrients to the river that help sustain the next generation.

◆

WADING OPTIONS

Working downstream from Keswick Dam, there are few wading opportunities in this upper reach until you get to the ACID Irrigation Dam. This structure backs up the water in the upper reach creating a deep, almost lake-like body of water for several miles. Just below the dam you can find numerous rock outcroppings to stand on and fish without entering the water.

Known locally as the "Posse Grounds" after the horse boarding facility just above, the area immediately behind the Redding Civic Auditorium can offer some great wading and fishing opportunities. The next major access point downstream is referred to as Turtle Bay and is considered a major bird sanctuary. The river for a brief time runs from west to east, and Turtle Bay is on the Civic Auditorium side of the river just before it turns in a southerly direction.

East Turtle Bay is across the river and downstream from Turtle Bay, just below the Hwy. 299-44 Bridge. Volunteers from Shasta Fly Fishers of Redding built a parking lot well away from the river here in an attempt to keep people from driving into the river to wash their vehicles. Numerous shallow riffles can be found in this area.

Wading anglers can fish the fast riffle below the Cypress Street Bridge from the west side of the river. Although often wadable, this is not wading for the faint of heart. So bring a wading staff and fight the current. There are plenty of big trout in this section.

Below Cypress Street wading access is limited due to deeper water and private property. The next easy access downstream is the area around the Sacramento's confluence with Clear Creek on the west side. There are islands and gravel bars in this area, as well as some magnificent fish. There is a fisherman's access parking lot at the sewerage treatment plant below Clear Creek off Eastside Road. At the end of River Crest Drive just below there are ponds full of bass and bluegills with a good section of river behind it.

Knighton riffle and a great island area can be accessed off Knighton Road from the east side of the river. Park your car where you see the other cars and hike the easy path down to the river.

Anderson River Park is the next major access downstream on the west side of the river. It offers numerous spots to either wade or fish off the bank into shallow riffles. Just below the

park there is also access from the end of both Dodson and Shelly Lanes on the west side.

The last good wading access for an angler without a boat can be found below the Deschutes Bridge off the end of a road called Green Acres. You can fish around a great island across from where Cow Creek enters the Sacramento. There are lots of bald eagles in this area, especially during the winter season.

POPULAR FLOAT TRIPS

Much more of the lower Sac is available to anglers with boats. Not only do you have the option of fishing while you float, but you get access to lots of areas you cannot drive or wade to. The first boat launch ramp below Keswick Dam is in Caldwell Park, offering boat access to the upper river which is not easily waded. This is a scenic area where you will see few, if any, other anglers. Just across and below the ACID Irrigation Dam is a boat launch ramp at the Posse Grounds. Many people floating the upper river consider this one of the best places to put in.

It's an easy half-day of fishing to float from the Posse Grounds down to the next launch facility which is off Bonnyview Road on the west side of the river. The next boat access is quite a bit farther down on the east side of the river at the Sacramento River RV Park. There is a modest fee for using this facility.

The two remaining boat launch ramps in this popular wild trout section are at Anderson River Park and Balls Ferry. You can access Balls Ferry off Ash Creek Road on the east side of the river.

Depending on the types of water you prefer to float, some of the more popular trips are from the Posse Grounds to Bonnyview for a half-day, or to Sacramento River RV Park for an all-day experience. If you prefer to do more boat fishing and less wading, you might even go down as far as Anderson River Park. The lower run usually begins at the Bonnyview launch ramp and goes down to Balls Ferry. Several experienced local guides prefer this lower stretch for float trips in the winter months.

FALL AND WINTER FISHING ON THE LOWER SAC

ORANGE EGGS AND TINY GREEN BUGS

The lower Sacramento River offers angling opportunities 365 days a year, so the fun and challenge never end. But cool weather angling on the river is decidedly different than summertime since river flows, accessibility, flies and techniques all undergo a marked transformation. In order to keep up with this constantly changing ecosystem, the successful angler has to be willing to abandon trusted flies and techniques and approach the river with an open mind.

The first thing you will notice is that there's a lot less river. Depending on the year, flows from beneath Keswick Dam will drop from the 12,000 to 14,000 cfs range to 4,000 to 5,000

cfs, usually in mid-September. What had been previously a drift boat fishery transforms overnight into a wader-friendly river allowing almost limitless access. Gone are the days of having to give hard consideration to safety before entering the water, but another factor comes into play which begs the wading angler to be extremely careful before setting foot on the stream bottom.

PUTTING YOUR FOOT IN IT

The Sacramento River above Deschutes Bridge is managed as a sanctuary for spawning Chinook salmon. Almost constantly during the cooler months the river is host to many thousands of huge, ocean-bright salmon building redds, or nests, on every suitable shallow gravel bar in the river. You can almost see the conflict coming.

Too often well-meaning anglers in the throws of fish fever look at the opportunity to catch egg-gorging trout behind the salmon redds without noticing they are tramping all over the redds. And we might as well come clean. Fly fishers are no better about this than anyone else.

Salmon redds look like round depressions in the gravel two to three feet across. They are slightly deeper in the middle giving them a dish-like appearance. There does not have to be salmon in the redd for it to contain fertilized eggs. When in doubt, avoid wading through these areas.

Like the native Wintu people who sustained themselves off this rich fishery, modern anglers have learned the obvious value in dropping single egg fly patterns behind spawning salmon. But the takes are often surprisingly delicate. When a trout spies a drifting egg pattern, it isn't as if the egg will try to escape. for the trout it's a sure thing. Why "bust a fin" when a leisurely sip will do just as well? Pay attention. By "matching the hatch" with fly patterns designed to imitate salmon eggs modern anglers   still experience tremendous success.

A WINTER WONDERLAND

California's big claim to fame is predicable weather and this December morning is no exception. Big surprise, it's about 45 degrees and drizzling. On the one hand it is not the most appealing morning weather but, on the other, an entree to some of the wildest big-fish dry fly fishing of the year.

Cagey Lower Sac anglers know the signs and just what to look for. It's all about Baetis, that tiny godsend of an insect seemingly created as an antidote to wintertime cabin fever. Also known as the blue winged olive, this little mayfly proliferates on days that are just nasty. First you need cool temperatures. If there's too much wind they are blown off the water before the trout can pick them off the surface. Drizzle is best, but if it gets raining too hard the trout cannot see the bugs. So if you can just get a day where these conditions line up, and the moon, perhaps, is in the seventh house, these bugs will carpet the surface and turn the trout fanatic.

Now this isn't as simple as you might think. The way it usually progresses, your first time out you will hit conditions perfectly and bring so many trout to hand that you might be tempted to feel a bit guilty. But after a few more times out you will begin to understand the cruel hoax. The best practical advice in the absence of rising trout is to fish a #14 Pheasant Tail Nymph on 4X tippet six feet under a yarn strike indicator.

My first experience with this phenomenon found Garth and I meeting around lunch time just below Clear Creek. He headed downstream toward a certain gravel bar he likes to fish this time of the year. He is content to swing nymphs through this water all day and has been known to land some pretty impressive fish. It is classic trout water and the river opens up here revealing stunning views of Mount Shasta to the north and Mount Lassen to the east. While Garth headed down toward what I'm sure he considered to be a sure thing, I decided to explore some of the slower side channels above Clear Creek.

There is one thing about fishing with Garth that he would never admit in a million years. Fact is, it really gets him when he doesn't catch the most or biggest fish. Mind you, he would never say anything. It's more of a sullen, sulky attitude. In his defense, Garth is without a doubt an expert fisherman. There are plenty of times I've seen him nail one fish after another with a deft skill that will take me many more years to master. But he's also an "around the next bend" kind of guy. There have been a few too many times when, after fishing just out of my sight, the proportions and staggering numbers of fish he's allegedly caught far surpass even his considerable ability. Now it was my turn.

Maybe it was the rotten weather or the fact that the water I was exploring was unfamiliar to me. Instead of picking a likely spot and fishing a nymph, I walked a bit further than I might normally have. I could see the disturbance in the water from a distance and the dive-bombing antics of five or six swallows suggested there might be a hatch coming off in the slick between two islands. It turned out the water here was literally carpeted with Baetis mayflies and the trout were responding like a pack of ravenous bluefish.

The bugs had pale olive bodies in about a size 16 and the slightly longish slate-colored wings swept back like the masts of tiny sailboats. I had an imitation that would do, but the challenge was to get the trout to choose my fly in the presence of so many thousands of naturals. The odds were kind to me that day and in several hours I was able to catch and release 14 good trout, the largest an honest 22 inches.

I don't remember whether the hatch died down or I just decided I'd had enough fun for one day, but Garth was waiting by my car when I called it quits. I handily got him to admit catching two trout of, as he put it, "at least 16 inches." "Stretching it," I thought. Milking it for all it was worth I engaged in some inane small talk totally unrelated to fishing since I knew it would drive him crazy. Finally, when he could contain himself no more, I let him have the truth.

I think it was Robert Traver who said fishing was the most fun you could have outside of the bedroom. He obviously never met Garth.